BLACK N BLUE BOYS

BROKEN MEN

BLACK N BLUE BOYS / BROKEN MEN

DAEL ORLANDERSMITH

SOFT SKULL PRESS
NEW YORK

Library of Congress Cataloging-in-Publication Data
Orlandersmith, Dael.
  Black n blue boys / broken men / Dael Orlandersmith.
    pages cm
Summary: "In the spirit of *Push* by Sapphire. Bold, beautiful and fierce—Dael Orlandersmith delivers a riveting story in *Black n Blue Boys / Broken Men*. This gritty, one-man play portrays five unforgettable male characters, linked by their efforts to forge identities in families fractured by abuse. Each relates a story that transforms these challenges into a celebration of our capacity to survive. Orlandersmith created this piece after working at a shelter for homeless youth in the 1980s, and her writing brings these characters roaring to life. At once powerful and heartbreakingly poetic, *Black n Blue Boys / Broken Men* will leave you breathless." —Provided by publisher.

ISBN 978-1-59376-532-3 (pbk.)
1. Men—Drama. 2. Abusive parents—Drama. I. Title. II. Title: Broken men.
PS3565.R5734B57 2013
812'.54—dc23
                                    2013017906

Cover design by Nina Tara
Interior Design by Sabrina Plomitallo-González, Neuwirth & Associates

SOFT SKULL PRESS
New York, NY
www.softskull.com

Printed in the United States of America

Production History

BLACK N BLUE BOYS / BROKEN MEN was
co-commissioned and co-produced by The Goodman
Theatre (Robert Falls, Artistic Director; Roche Schulfer,
Executive Director) and Berkeley Repertory Theatre
(Tony Taccone, Artistic Director; Susan Medak,
Managing Director). The play had its world premiere
at the Berkeley Repertory Theatre on May 30, 2012,
performed by Dael Orlandersmith, under the direction
of Chay Yew. Set design was by Daniel Ostling; costume
design by Anita Yavich; lighting design by Ben Stanton;
and sound design by Mikhail Fiksel. The production
dramaturgs were Madeleine Oldham and Tanya Palmer

BLACK N BLUE BOYS / BROKEN MEN subsequently
premiered at The Goodman Theatre on October 7, 2012,
with the same cast and artistic staff.

SCENES

Mike
Flaco
Larry
Ian
Timmy
Flaco
Tenny
Ian
Mike
Epilogue

(Characters are all male. Their ages range from eleven to sixty. Each of them has had a history of abuse.)

(Stage should be bare except possibly for chairs and a table.)

(Piece can be performed by any gender or race. It can be performed by a single actor or multiple actors.)

MIKE

(*Actor moves into spotlight. Sits in a chair and becomes Mike.*)

I'm a writer and a social worker
I got my HS diploma / went to college

I DID THAT

I did NOT let what my parents did take that away from me

I remember this one fight they had . . . man this was a HORROR man / it really
was . . . she had given birth to my baby sister two weeks before / and both of
them had been drinking and she and she said (*imitates her*), "I need money"

He gave her money / and she said (*imitates her*), "This ain't enough for seven
kids—there's seven kids here" (*becomes self*) and he said (*imitates him*), "Well
ALL those motherfuckin kids ain't mine—that baby girl ain't mine—and there's
ONE I know for sure ain't mine" (*voice trails off*)

(*Becomes self*)

And

ANYTIME he said that / he looked at me

(*Beat*)

He went outside and was standing on the corner with some other guys / they
all had plastic cups and they were passing a bottle around between them in
a paper bag and I was about seven and I remember looking out the window /
looking at all of these guys but especially him

And

They were all wearing these loud colored suits / these played out popcorn
pimp suits / they wore their hats at a rakish angle / and they all got their
shoes from Regal Shoes stores / or Florsheim's / shiny patent leather shoes
or platforms

They're saying shit to all these young women walking past / a lot of the time
they don't even talk TO the women / they refer to a body part (*does a series*

of voices), "Oh man look at that ass / would love to ride that ass / would love to EAT her all night long"

(*Becomes self*)

They would look at the girl and say it while talking to each other as if she were an inanimate object

My mother would look out the window watchin' all this and she would say (*imitates her*), "Motherfucker I'll snatch you out your pants and I'll disconnect that bitch from her asshole"

Then she would sit at the kitchen table holding my baby sister and giving her a bottle and she was drinking and smoking cigarettes with a friend of hers and I said (*as if to her*), "Mom you shouldn't be smoking / it's not good for the baby and also you've been drinkin'—you may drop her"

(*Becomes self*)

And my older brother—he was home at the time and he said (*imitates him*), "Yeah Mom / Mike is right"

(*Becomes self*)

And she said (*imitates her*), "Let me tell you two no good lil NIGGAS something / YOU don't tell me SHIT / you don't tell me a fuckin thing" / (*becomes self*) then she looks at ME and said (*imitates her*), "SPECIALLY YOU NIGGA"

(*Becomes self*)

I HATE being called that—NIGGER—I HATE IT

They both called us that—NIGGER—and they called my sisters NIGGER BITCHES

(*Beat*)

So this day / he was standing on the corner drinkin' / she was inside sittin' at the table drinkin' / fuming / gassin' herself up / using what he said about me and my new little sister maybe not being his / I was watching her work herself up / she actually MADE herself breathe heavy / she was prepping herself / giving herself permission to drink more and fight him

She and her friend almost finished a fifth of scotch

It was about one o'clock in the afternoon

She handed my sister to her friend and she went outside with a butcher's knife. She stood at the top of the stoop.

We watched from the window as she yelled at him saying (*imitates her*), "NO GOOD NIGGA BASTARD / YOU THE ONLY NIGGA I BEEN WIT FOR EIGHT YEAR / HOW YOU GONNA SAY THAT BABY GIRL AIN'T YOURS"

(*Becomes self*)

He looked up at her and said (*imitates him*), "You need to take yo ass back in the house and stop fucking wit me"

(*Becomes self*)

And she is REALLY breathing heavy now and yells (*imitates her*), "FUCK YOU / YOU NO GOOD BLACK ASS MOTHERFUCKER"

(*Becomes self*)

She runs down the steps with a butcher's knife / and goes straight for him / some of the men try to stop her / but she swings the knife in their direction / they back away

(*Slight pause*)

They back away laughing

My father goes to grab her / she cuts him across the palm of his right hand / he jerks back raises left hand to block her again / he grabs her hand / she breaks loose / she goes to cut him across his torso / he jumps back and kicks her in the stomach / she goes down

He gets on top of her / grabs her by the hair / and slaps her face side to side

/ she's screaming / screaming her lungs out / some of his friends try to pull him off / but he shoves them back

Then

He bangs her head against the pavement screaming (*imitates him*), "I TOOK YO ASS IN WHEN NOBODY WANTED YOU / ALL THEM KIDS YOU GOT / YOU WAS OUT THERE HOIN' AND ON DOPE / I ACCEPTED THAT TRICK BABY MICHAEL / HOW MANY MEN WOULD DO THAT BITCH?"

(*Becomes self*)

My older brother looked down at me and said (*imitates him*), "Come on Mike / get away from the window"

(*Becomes self*)

Later that night I asked him, "What's a trick baby?"

My older brother said (*imitates him*), "It means a baby born from a ho / the father is one of the men she picks up for money"

(*Becomes self*)

And

I asked (*as if to him*), "Is that what I am?"

They all got quiet

My older brother said (*imitates him*), "Yeah Mike / that's what you are"

(*Back to audience, becomes self*)

I didn't fully understand what that meant—sex / I didn't know / I was seven but then again / I DID know

I saw the women standing outside the train station on Junius Street

I knew what they were doing was bad

Therefore

I knew I must ALSO be bad

(*Beat*)

But I knew there was MORE

I knew I didn't want to live like this

I KNEW that at SEVEN

I loved to read

I'd tried to stay away from the house as much as I could

I spent lots of time at the library

I would actually be excited to go

By the time I was ten / I read Charles Dickens and I thought, "Man, he lives just like me, except he's English"

Those words would hit me and I could see me and Pip running down Brooklyn streets hand in hand finding then beating DOWN my FAKE father and we'd laugh / sidestep / slide past the Artful Dodger and slap five

Later I read Claude Brown and Piri Tomas and tasted / smelled / walked Salsa / soul / bebop / hip-hop / ditty-bop NOISE

Even later

I read Dostoevsky understanding the need FOR SOMETHING PURE / understanding the need to kill to make it all PURE

I read them and knew I wasn't alone

I reached for THEM—THOSE writers when I got / slapped / kicked / punched and called NIGGER from them—my mother and HIM

I reached for them / wondering who my REAL father was

And

Did he know I existed?

I reached for THEM when my two brothers went to jail

I reached for THEM when two of my sisters got hooked on drugs and when the youngest one got lost in the bottle

I kept REACHING FURTHER
Tolstoy
Baldwin
Morrison
Henry James

When I reached for THEM I was in Brooklyn but I was also BEYOND Brooklyn / I was BEYOND rat-filled tenements and popcorn pimps and nickel-and-dime whores and worn-down rattling train stations / I reached for them / kept reaching for them and others / I kept reaching and reaching and KNEW I was not a NIGGER TRICK BABY / I was NOBODY'S NIGGER / I was NOT

I was BEYOND

I KNEW I was gonna write about kids like me

I KNEW by writing about kids like that it would help kids like me

I KNEW I would NEVER treat a kid the way I was treated

I KNEW

(*Beat*)

By the time I was fifteen / HE had left for good and mother was NEVER sober and would say (*imitates her*), "ALL that money you makin' / you ain't bringin' none in heah / he left me 'cause a YOU / 'cause you wasn't HIS"

(*Becomes self*)

I see her / I hear her but I'm BEYOND her

My English teacher helps me with colleges and I get into City College

I get into a private room at the dorm

(*Slight pause*)

It was like having my own apartment

It was INCREDIBLE

It was my OWN space and I filled it with books

And

Even though I was a full-time student and working part time / I still wrote

I wrote poems/stories about Brooklyn

I dug into those words trying the make the stink of booze come on to the paper itself

I wanted to use words so the feel of slaps and punches would jump off the page

I tried to arrange/rearrange those words to picture the man that planted his seed in my mother

How he did it?

I used words to try to imagine him throwing money on that BED

Or

UP against a wall in a Brooklyn hallway

Or

In the backseat of some broken-down car in front of the Junius Street train station

(*Slight pause*)

I became the editor for the school literary magazine, *The Promethean*, and everyone was taken by the stories

They called me the "NEW Baldwin" or the "black Charles Dickens"

(*Beat*)

I graduate

The world is OPEN

NOTHING can get in the way

(*Beat*)

I get a job in a runaway shelter / I'm doing counseling / I'm doing intakes / I'm also reading my work to the kids / doing writing workshops with the kids and you hear/see how angry they are

You hear it / see it in THEIR words and a lot of the time they take it out on you (*slight pause*) ME / they take it out on ME but I understand

I told the kids about my being a TRICK BABY

And

One of them said (*does a voice*), "Yo damn Mike / I got it bad but NOT like you / I'm so sorry man"

(*Becomes self*)

I would read what I wrote to kids in the center and they would say (*imitates a voice*), "Damn Mike / that's just the way the way it is / that's the way I FEEL man"

(*Becomes self*)

I'm sending my work out

I get rejected but keep sending

This goes on for a while

I run writing workshops with the kids and sometimes they can't / don't partic-ipate in the workshops because they're too angry / their stays are temporary / some are there for a few days / then you never see them again / or someone is put there for a month until they get into a permanent group home / only to run away from that group home after YOU helped get them there

You see the black eyes and swollen faces from their parents

You see the black eyes and swollen faces from pimps/johns

You see swollen arms from shooting drugs

You see teenaged kids who are HIV-positive

And/or pregnant

You see how bitter beat they are and you know you cannot take it personally and you gotta keep on keeping on

There are days you get totally worn down/out but you gotta keep keeping on

---

FLACO

(*Nuyorican, fifteen, talking to social worker about his past.*)

You know it's all a hustle to me yo / know what I sayin'? / Like it's ALL a hustle / I mean / I mean you sit there and you gotta hustle to get me into a group home or whatever / you gotta up my rep / make me look good / not tell people about me being violent 'cause you gotta place me, *¿verdad?*

(*Beat*)

I mean you know how may group homes I been in, man?

I been in eleven group homes since I was ten years old

My brother has been in seven foster homes

I been in the system for five years

Five years man! And I'm only fifteen

YOU SOCIAL WORKERS AND COUNSELORS said that you were gonna help

That you were gonna get me out but you and all of you ended up lyin'

Lyin' like you always do

You lie 'cause you hustle

You gotta make that trick

You gotta PIMP ME

You PIMP me to make YOU look good

You gotta sell me to the system

You gotta lie and tell them I'm good so you can get me placed / get the MONEY to get me placed / lessen your caseload / so you can go home and get some rest

YOU gotta sell that that lie—ME / I'm the LIE and you gotta smile while doing it

You gotta know who that trick is real fast and how to tap that trick and keep smiling

You GOTTA be social

Me and you—we're BOTH social workers man

Gotta turn that trick baby

Maybe I'm telling you the truth o maybe I'm lyin'

Layin' down my hustle

(*Beat*)

Look at you

Look at you lookin' at me

(*Moves in closer*)

You like what you see?

Like what you see, ¿*mi amor?*

You want me

¿*Me quieres?*

¿*Quieres mi culo?*

(*The social worker tells Flaco to stop speaking this way*)

(*Slyly*)

Okay—awright I'll stop / I promise I'll stop *pero* the look in your eyes man made me think—you know?

I mean I KNOW the look

I know the LOOK well

¿Tu sabes?

But I was wrong / so I'll be cool

MAYBE I was wrong / so I'll stop

(*Beat*)

(*To counselor*)

I really did believe YOU people man

I used to believe in PEOPLE

I really did man

I was stupid for believing adults in general man because ALL OF YOU LIE. All this (*imitates a voice*) "I PROMISE YOU IT WILL BE FINE" (*becomes self*) shit y'all say. All o y'all are a buncha bitches man and I don't care if you don't like me callin' you that man

I used to believe in family

I mean bein' there in that house man with her—my mother man and my pops—man that shit was fucked up and everybody knew that it was fucked up. Poppy would get into his Chivas talking about Puerto Rico and how one day we're gonna leave Coney Island and get out the projects and see San Juan

He'd say (*imitates him*), "*La playa aqui hijos*—it ain't real / this Coney Island beach—it ain't real / the water in PR is PURE/CLEAN"

(*Becomes self*)

Then he would take me and my brother Marco under each arm and bring us to the window and he'd say (*imitates him*), "Take a look at the water out there but don't see it as Coney Island—see it as Puerto Rico / if you really look / if you REALLY look PAST it / you can see San Juan / Santurce"

(*Becomes self*)

And me and my little brother Marco—we would look / squint our eyes and say (*does this*), "Yeah Poppy I see Santurce / I REALLY see it / when we goin' Poppy / when you gonna take us!" And he always said (*imitates him*), "Soon *hijo* / soon" (*becomes self*) my mother—she would say (*imitates her*), "Why you telling them that! *Coño* you can't even get enough money together to take the fucking subway!" (*becomes self*) and Poppy would say (*imitates him*), "Baby don't talk like that, you gotta believe in me babe," and she would say (*imitates her*), "I used to / I used to and nuthin' changed / nuthin'" (*becomes self*) his head would drop / he couldn't take her being mean to him / he loved her—my moms—he really did

She would get violent sometimes and just for no reason jump on him / then scratch his face or she would grab a knife and one time she did cut him you know? And he forgave her man

I mean FORGAVE her for doin' that man / made excuses for her all the time (*imitates father*), "Hey Mommy's fiery you know / real fiery"

(*Beat*)

He tried to get me and Marco to get close to her / Marco—he REALLY tried *pero* it didn't work and Marco would cry and say (*imitates him*), "Mommy please don't push me away / I love you" (*becomes self*) and she would push him away and she would scream and scream

She would tell us (*imitates her*), "I HATE YOU I HATE YOU and they're telling me that I should kill you!" (*becomes self*) and we would get scared and say (*as if to her*), "Who Mommy? Who's telling you to kill us?" (*back to audience*) and she would say (*imitates her*), "The Daisy Chain People tell me / they tell me that you and Marco keep me from them / they want to hold me / kiss me / make me feel good / they say you and Marco take time away from me so I should kill you both

(*Becomes self, beat*)

I was ten and Marco was six when she started doing this and by the time Poppy came home from work—she'd be okay / I tried to ask Poppy about the Daisy Chain People and he would look at me and say (*imitates him*), "Oh no! Mommy's being fiery again—lissen Poppa / it'll take care of her (*becomes self*) but I could tell the way he looked that he KNEW / he KNEW Mommy was sick

He didn't want to see it / he loved her that much

(*Beat*)

Poppy was a super in a school and he would get up to get us dressed / give us breakfast and get us to school and when he got out of his job he would come and pick us up / I heard him tell my aunt—his sister—that Mommy needed (*sarcastically*) looking after. Again she was always actin' weird / talking to people that weren't there but there were times she could control it / YOU social workers / counselors whatever you call yourselves say it's (*sarcastically*) "part of her sickness" BUT I KNOW there were times she coulda controlled that shit / I fuckin KNOW (*beat*) so yeah Poppy was doing EVERYTHING. Getting us up for school / cooking dinner when he got home

This one day after school I had made me and Marco a sandwich and I was watchin' TV and Marco was sleepin' and I heard her talking to the people that only she saw and heard and then she yelled at me (*imitates her*), "Flaco get out here NOW"

(*Becomes self*)

So I go the living room man and she's looking at me and her eyes are bulgin' and she got this real long knife and she says (*imitates her*), "The Daisy Chain King—he's my REAL husband / he's telling me to kill you" (*becomes self*) and I say, "No mommy PLEASE / PLEASE Mommy" and I say (*as if to her*), "Tell him—tell the Daisy Chain King I'm not a bad boy (*looks away*), so she comes toward me holding the knife and I'm scared shit man and then she traces the knife over my face / neck / my stomach / back again to my face / neck / she does this a few times (*pause*). Then she says (*imitates her*), "Pull down your pants" (*becomes self*) and I take them down (*pause*) then she says (*imitates her*), "Take off your underwear" (*becomes self*) so I take off my underwear she touches my thing sayin' (*imitates her*), "The Daisy Chain King says I can touch YOU / I can use YOU to get ready for HIM / for the day I become Daisy Chain Queen"

(*Pause, becomes self*)

And I get hard

I get real hard and I say (*as if to her*), "Mommy stop / please STOP / I don't like this"

(*Looks away*)

I didn't like IT but part of me DID

Part of me loved IT

Part of me wanted IT so BAD

I hated that I wanted IT

I couldn't control IT

And she says (*imitates her*), "You want me to stop but you getting hard" (*becomes self*) and she laughs / she laughs at me

It happened for like three months

I didn't tell Poppy

I didn't know HOW to tell him

This one day / she got naked and made me get on top of her . . . (*voice trails off*)

I told Poppy and he looked at me

Then

He said (*imitates him*), "Flaco / she didn't touch you LIKE THAT / she's YOUR
MOTHER Flaco (*becomes self*) and I say (*as if to him*), "Poppy she DID / she's
SICK Poppy / everybody around the projects says / she don't never leave the
house (*back to audience*) and again he says (*imitates him*), "SHE IS YOUR
MOTHER Flaco / she did NOT do that / MEN are the ones that touch kids
nasty / women give birth / they don't do that / your mother / *mi esposa*
didn't do that / STOP it"

(*Becomes self, beat*)

One day she was standin' by the elevator and there was this kid on my floor
/ he was twelve and he was waiting for the elevator to go downstairs and
she was only wearing a nightgown / she lifted the nightgown and told him
to touch her

He ran inside and his moms came out and beat her and next thing you know
all these women jumped on her and they ALL were hittin' her

I tried to stop it but I couldn't

I ran to Tee Tee's house and she called the police and Poppy

The ambulance and police came and Mommy was smiling / she kept saying
(*imitates her*), "The King loves me / he loves me / he's more than the Daisy
Chain King / he's a god / He's GOD / GOD loves me

(*Becomes self*)

By now we were all outside and people was pointing / looking and laughing

Poppy went inside and got her coat

Marco had me by the hand and was crying

A cop—he seemed real nice / he came over to me and said (*imitates him*),
"Flaco / what happened?"

(*Becomes self*)

And I told him what she did and Poppy heard me

He comes over screaming / he said (*imitates him*), "YOUR MOTHER DIDN'T
TOUCH YOU LIKE THAT / HOW CAN YOU SAY THAT ABOUT YOUR OWN
MOTHER / MY WIFE"

(*Becomes self*)

And I say (*as if to him*), "POPPY SHE NEEDS HELP / SHE DID TOUCH ME LIKE
THAT / LOOK WHAT SHE DID WITH THE KID IN OUR BUILDING / MAYBE
SHE WOULD HAVE GOTTEN MARCO"

(*Speaks outwardly*)

And AGAIN he said (*imitates him*), "YOU MADE THEM TAKE HER FROM ME
/ I WAS GONNA GET US TO PR / SHE DID NOT TOUCH YOU OR THAT BOY
/ SHE GETS EMOTIONAL / THAT'S ALL / SHE'S FIERY BUT NOT LIKE THAT /
NOT LIKE THAT WE CAN'T GO TO PR BECAUSE OF YOU"

(*Beat*)

The next day / I'm sittin' in a shrink's office—this woman—and she's asking me
all these questions. Wearing a whole lotta makeup and perfume / you could
tell she was *una vieja pero* / she was still trying to be young

She just kept looking at me

She got to the part about Mommy touchin' me

I mean I COULD see the look on her face when she got to THAT part / I could
SEE how she was tryin' NOT to be shocked and she FINALLY said (*imitates
her*), "Flaco / it says here your mother touched you but I think the way it's
written—there MUST be a mistake" (*becomes self*) and THEN I DO decide to
talk and say (*as if to her*), "WHY? Why would that be a mistake?" (*back to
audience*) and she says (*imitates her*), "It says here MOLESTATION" (*back to
being self*) and I say, "What's that?" (*back to audience*) and she says (*imitates
her*), "Well that is what MEN do to girls / women or young boys" (*becomes

self) and I say (*as if to her*), "You mean like putting their dicks in them?" (*back to audience*) and she says (*imitates her*), "Yes / that's exactly what I mean" (*becomes self*) and I say (*as if to her*), "Well my moms ain't got no dick but yeah she touched me like that" (*back to audience*) and she says (*imitates her*), "I'm sure you mistook how she touched you / I'm NOT saying that she didn't touch you but women / MOTHERS don't touch their children like this"

(*Becomes self*)

So molestation is what men do to boys or girls

And I tell her—this bitch—this and of course because she was a woman / she got REAL mad at ME and it was like she wanted to RUMBLE with me man and she kept saying (*imitates her*), "Flaco / you are VERY young / you can misinterpret things," (*back to being self*) and I tell her (*as if to her*), "I KNOW I'm a kid but I'm telling you the truth / she may be my mother but she did DO that"

I started screaming

I ran around the office screaming

People were trying to grab me and finally someone did

(*Pause*)

They bring me to hospital and I'm fighting the doctor and then next you know / all these nurses and people are trying to hold me down

All these faces

All these adult faces

All of them dressed in white

And then all of them HELD ME down

I felt something sting

A needle goes into my arm

Then everything went black

(*Beat*)

Then I get sent to the first of the eleven group homes I end up runnin' from man

LARRY

(*White, early sixties, originally from Brooklyn, sweeping leaves in Central Park, watching a group of men and their sons play touch football, there's the sound of people playing in the park.*)

Jeezus some of the stuff ya find / unbelievable / you wouldn't believe the things people do / stuff I find / jeezus people are so nasty / and the stuff ya see

Like people havin' sex in the OPEN / goin' to bathroom in the OPEN—nasty—excuse my language—nasty bastards. . . . there are also people who live here / camp out here / homeless and some of 'em are nice and I kinda turn my back you know—don't tell anybody 'cause some of 'em are good people who are just down on their luck / Central Park is so beautiful (*pronounces it "beautiful"*)

Why do people wanna make it ugly? / It's a great park (*suddenly looks towards the field*) whoa—look at that kid run / he can really run / he's got it! / He's really got it this time TOUCHDOWN!—way to go!

WOW! Now I tell ya / THAT was something!

So the kid got the touchdown

He FINALLY got it

He was workin' so HARD to make it

(*Sweeps a little but still looking towards the field*)

(*Stops sweeping*)

Ya know that kid / his older brother and father come here every Saturday and play football / they been comin'—jeez I don't know—what like four years?

Oh I see all kinds of people / I notice all the people that come into the park

Some I know by name / others by sight

And you know a lot of them know me too

Some people call me the mayor of Central Park / they say (*does a voice*), "Hey Mayor Larry!"

(*Becomes self*)

People can be real nice

BUT

a lotta time people don't notice me but that's okay

(*Looks at the boy again*)

Like this kid NOW—well he's a young man now—he don't know me

(*Shakes his head*)

That Father and older brother of his—they always ran him hard, ya know?

―――――――――

I'm lookin' at this guy and can tell he went to some Ivy League school and he's some kinda lawyer/stockbroker type and his wife runs up his charge card

I see him joggin' a lot too

The father—he's not young but he thinks by all that joggin' he does it's gonna keep him young

I see him tryin' to pick up young girls on the joggers' trail

And

I see the girls exchange looks and laugh at him behind his back

The young girls call him CHICKEN NECK

You know how as you get older / the skin around your throat sags?

Well this guy has a saggy neck

If he ever says somethin' to me nasty that's what I'll call him / I'll say, "SCREW YOU CHICKEN NECK" / but again why would he notice a guy like me?

He's arrogant that guy—so full of himself

(*Picks up the broom and swings it a little*)

I'd like to hit him with this . . .

(*Beat*)

You know four years ago is when I first noticed them

I remember seein' a whole bunch of them—friends of the father and their wives and kids and they all seemed to be having a good time / and I was trimming some hedges and I looked over and saw the younger son turning rope for some girls playin' double dutch / and the women were sittin' under this tree talking / sunbathin' / eatin' and all the guys—except for the young guy—were on the field playin' Frisbee and softball . . .

Next you thing you know / this SCREAM comes from center field and the father comes runnin' towards the younger son and when he gets to him / he yanks the rope out his hands and says (*imitates him*), "NO / THIS GAME IS FOR GIRLS / UNDERSTAND / YOU DON'T PLAY THIS / GET ON THE FIELD NOW!"

(*Becomes self*)

I mean this guy was REALLY pissed off about this—really

And even the other guys were telling him that it was no big deal and—this woman / I guess it mighta been the wife, said (*imitates her*), "Oh come on—you're overreactin'"

(*Becomes self*)

This guy just looked at her and said (*imitates him*), "Look he's A MAN / maybe I'm old fashioned—too bad / he needs to act like a MAN and I'm gonna see that he does."

(*Becomes self*)

So

Yeah after that / I would see them on the field a lot on Saturdays

The father and the older brother would throw footballs as hard as they could knocking the poor kid down / they'd toss Frisbees as high and fast as they could makin' the kid run

I never once saw that kid enjoy himself

I mean when you come to Central Park it's supposed to be fun

For FOUR years / they pushed and shoved and bullied that kid

Many times they'd do it in front of the other guys / I'd hear the father say to the older son (*imitates him*), "You and ME will MAKE him into a man / I CAN'T BE EMBARRASSED"

(*Becomes self, incredulously*)

HE can't be embarrassed huh?

Jeezus!—excuse my language—what an asshole

What a real asshole

And the older brother is an asshole too

How could he treat his own brother like that?

The stuff this guy is teachin' his sons . . .

Just cause someone has a kid—it don't make them a parent—ya know?

(*Sweeps again*)

Well that kid—he showed 'em today

He really showed 'em

Man—it was great! TOUCHDOWN

He made a TOUCHDOWN

I guess they made him a "MAN"

IAN

(*Late thirties, English-Irish/Oasis's "Force of Nature" plays as a loop.*)

(*Please note! Irish accent is specifically from Belfast.*)

Nothing can hold you back, nothing can get in your way except for you

Look at me, I come from three generations of Irish / Scottish drunken pint glass philosophers whose only function was to get and stay pissed and give their ninety-proof advice while falling off of a pub stool . . .

Then

They staggered home / beat their wives and kids

Passed out

Hungover of course the next morning—apologetic the next morning / can't remember the night before and begging forgiveness only to do it again

My father, my Da is of that lineage

Sitting in the pub talking about how great the sixties were / how great a singer he was / IS / how he (*sarcastically*) ALMOST made it to AMERICA

He got from Belfast to Manchester—or *Mad*chester as we call it—and no further

And when he gets in it—the whiskey / there's no turning back / and when he's in it there's no telling what's going to happen or how it will (*imitates father*) "talk to me / make me do things / say things that I don't mean" (*becomes self*) it—the whiskey—may soften him / make him nostalgic / or he may become belligerent

The stories and the reactions are ALWAYS completely different EACH time / he gets in the pub and then come the stories about meeting John Lennon and how John heard him play and said to him (*imitates him*), "Join us / be the fifth Beatle / we're going on tour in the States"

(*Becomes self*)

Or maybe it was Van Morrison who wanted him to go on tour to the States or maybe Wilson Pickett wanted him to be in his band and called him his "Irish Soul Brother" and EVERYONE in the pub is enthralled

Sometimes he made me go with him to the pub because he KNEW he would get pissed and needed someone to get him home and that someone had to be ME / during the week / he drank less / would have a few pints which is why he thought he wasn't a drunk (*imitates him*), "I fookin work / NEVER miss work / yew've food in yew/ I pay for the flat / clothes are on yer back / I'm entitled to a bit o' fun / to hell with youse"

(*Becomes self*)

Then of course he gets home LATE yelling at Mum / beating Mum because the food is cold (*slight pause*) he'd beat me too

(*Beat*)

I was raised in the council flats and Saturday night in the council flats—I mean it can get mad / REALLY mad. All these drunk adults and they're fighting / pissed out of their skulls because it's Saturday night and they can't go anywhere because there's no money / and they can't do anything because there's no money and that's the one night that's built up in songs and movies / where all the promises are made / you fall in love on Saturday night / you dance it ALL away on Saturday night / the whole week is geared towards Saturday night / nothing matters except Saturday night / but you're still in the council flat Saturday night and that can't be sung or drunk away

There was this one Saturday night / Da was in the pub from midday to closing / the barman called to say that Da needed (*sarcastically imitates him*) "looking after and can't make it back by himself" (*becomes self*) it was cold that night / I mean freeze-your-bollocks kind of cold / and I told Mum / I said (*as if to her*), "Mum it's cold / don't want to go" / (*back to audience*) and she says (*imitates her*), "Ian—he's yer Da" (*becomes self, back to audience*) / Mum kept after me but I did NOT go to the pub

(*Beat*)

So we're waiting for Da and we're scared out of our wits—especially me because I refused to get him and we hear him before we lay eyes on him /

we hear him singing "Dead End Street" by the Kinks / and we look out the window and he can barely stand / a mate of his has walked him home

As I look out the window / I'm petrified / I KNOW I'm going get it / and as his mate is trying to get Da up the stairs / I'm watching by the curtain praying Da would just pass out when he gets inside

I'm listening to his walk—that long short unsteady walk

His mate gets him in the flat

Da looks down at me and says (*imitates him*), "Yew lil cunt / Yew didn't come fer me" (*becomes self, back to audience*) he yanks me up and proceeds to slap me about / Mum jumps in / with one hand he slaps her down to the floor

Then

Da throws open the door and drags me outside / holds me over the landing by the collar and I'm screaming / BLOODY SCREAMING / WAILING and some people come out of their flats and they're saying (*imitates a voice*), "NO MATE! / PUT THE CHILD DOWN MATE! / DON'T!"

(*Becomes self*)

And

By now / almost EVERYBODY has come out of their flats and some are looking up and others down and Da is STILL holding me but NOW he is taking in ALL the people around him. He's holding me and taking them ALL in

A smile comes over his face

All these people have become his audience and he's smiling and holding me up to the crowd now / he's actually holding me up / as if I were on display and he's really smiling now and he says / announces to the crowd (*imitates him*), "I'M HIS DA / HE DIDN'T LISSEN TO ME / YER KIDS HAVE TO LISSEN TO YEW / IF YEW HAVE TO GIVE THEM A KICKING / GIVE THEM A KICKING!"

(*Becomes self*)

Then he says to me (*imitates him*), "SAY YER NUTTIN" (*becomes self*) and I say, "NO! NO I WON'T!"

_____

One bloke says (*imitates voice*), "OKAY MATE / YOU'RE RIGHT / YOU GOTTA DISCIPLINE—YOU'RE RIGHT BUT YOU'RE BEIN' A BIT ROUGH NOW MATE / I MEAN HE'S LITTLE"

(*Becomes self*)

And Da says to this man (*imitates him*), "NO! IN IRELAND WE KNEW TO MIND OUR PARENTS / WE KNEW / PEOPLE HERE IN ENGLAND KNOW NUTTIN OF DISCIPLINE—NUTTIN / WE MAY BE IN THIS GODFORSAKEN SHITE COUNTRY BUT HE WILL MIND ME / AND I WILL MAKE HIM MIND ME / IF I HAVE TO KICK HIM ALL NIGHT LONG / HE WILL MIND ME / I AM THE MAN IN MY HOUSE / HE TINKS HE KNOWS IT ALL BUT HE IS STUPID"

(*Becomes self*)

He keeps calling me stupid

And all these kids were crying / beggin' their parents to do something

It was like they were also crying for themselves

(*Beat*)

And Da by now is thinking he is IT / ALL eyes were on him NOW / he is a STAR and I finally break down and say, "I'm NUTTIN DA / NUTTIN / I'M NUTTIN!"

And he says (*imitates him*), "WHAT WAS THAT STUPID? WANT TO MAKE SURE I HEARD YEW RIGHT STUPID? / SAY IT SO EVERYONE CAN HEAR YEW"

(*Becomes self*)

And I say it again (*as if to father*), "I'M NUTTIN DA / NUTTIN"

(*Becomes self, back to audience*)

And

He says calmly / so fucking calmly (*imitates him*), "That's right yer NUTTIN and don't yew ever forget that"

(*Becomes self*)

Da drops me

He drops me from the second landing stairwell to the first

I crash onto the first stairwell

Mum rushes past Da to me and some neighbors come as well

The other kids and ME were screaming

ALL OF US KIDS were screaming

I heard one kid tell his da (*imitates a voice*), "Why didn't you stop that man Dad / WHY?"

(*Becomes self*)

And

The da said (*imitates him*), "Shut it / it has nuthin' to do with us"

(*Becomes self*)

Everyone goes back inside

Da goes to the fridge and gets a lager / then goes to the sitting room / drinks it and passes out while sitting in the chair

(*Slight pause*)

He sleeps there the whole night

When he wakes up the next morning / SUNDAY morning—it's all quiet, right?

The people who fought last night and drank last night—they're either sleeping it off or going to church to absolve themselves

It's an act of contrition

They're going to church to give themselves permission to get pissed and fight the following week

Because it WILL happen again and does happen every week

Friday and Saturday

Drinking / fighting

Sunday

feeling guilty about drinking and fighting and then going to the priest for absolution

(*Slight pause*)

But

THIS Sunday Da didn't go 'cause he was too hungover. Mum took me to Mass and when we got back / he took one look at my face—the left side was swollen—and he then looked down and closed his eyes. He KNEW it was the WORST beating he ever gave me / Mum told him what he'd done / he couldn't remember all of it—or so he said and he then goes to reach for me and I scream (*as if to him*), "DON'T TOUCH ME / I HATE YOU!"

THEN

He went to Mum and she pulled away from him sayin', (*imitates her*), "Serves yew right"

(*Becomes self*)

He goes into the sitting room and collapses into his chair and he's sobbing / sobbing his fuckin eyes out

Mum is looking at him saying (*imitates her*), "I should fookin leave yew / should take Ian and fookin leave yew / yew no good bastard yew" (*becomes self*) and Da is begging Mum / begging her not to leave / so he crawls across the floor to Mum and he grabs her around the waist and he is NOW WAILIN' (*imitates him*), "PLEASE don't leave me / PLEASE / won't do it again luv / please / love yew / love Ian / PLEASE / I would kill meself if youse left me"

(*Becomes self*)

Mum doesn't hug him but she doesn't push him away either

Then Mum holds him and Da he's kissing Mum

and he and Mum go into their room and they close the door . . . (*voice trails off*)

(*Beat*)

I made a decision

I decided that I would NO longer cry

I wouldn't cry in front of HIM

And

I would stay out if I felt like it

So

I did

I would stay out and he would beat me and I wouldn't cry / he got SO angry / and he even said (*imitates him*), "Yer a hard stupid bastard are yew? (*becomes self*) and I said (*as if to him*), "Go ahead Da or I can get the belt if you like / you do what you need to" (*back to audience*) and he just looked at me

(*Beat*)

By the time I was fourteen / I KNEW I had to get OUT

Get away from him AND Mum

Away from the flats

(*Beat*)

I stayed to myself

I went to school / I came home, studied

I got a part-time job

A couple of the boys around the flats tried to start a row

I fought back

No one bothered me afterwards

In the flats—you HAVE prove yourself

I also made an effort to lose my accent

I would watch telly and listen to how people spoke

I would borrow tapes from the library

And alcohol was OUT

I would NOT ever do that

NEVER

I was REPULSED by it

Worse than that—

Disgusted—was disgusted by it

(*Beat*)

Da would look at me and sneer (*imitates him*), "Not a bit of Celt in yew / you're a real ENGLISH man / wit all yer schoolin' yer still STUPID

(*Pause*)

By the time I was eighteen / I had enough

I had gotten through school

I decide to go to London and Mum is beggin' me not to go and Da is sayin' (*imitates him*), "He up and leaves his Mum and does not care a shite about me / selfish yew are / fookin selfish"

(*Becomes self*)

So the day I leave / Da is drunk—it was a Saturday so he started getting pissed midday and I packed all my gear and Mum had whiskey in her too and was well pissed / she said she needed it to (*mocks her*) "cheer her." Mum is hugging me and crying and I can't stand it—the smell of the whiskey IN HER / her skin clammy / I can't stand HER—the STENCH of HER / Da says (*imitates him*), "Give us the key / yer no longer welcome here / don't come back

(*Becomes self*)

And I take the key and throw it in his face and it cuts across his eye

He gets up / as if to hit me

I look back at him smiling but my eyes were hard

I made my eyes so hard

He backed down

(*Moves to another part of the stage / the Clash's "London Calling" comes on*)

And then I get to London

I work in a posh restaurant on the West End

I watch / listen to the customers that talk down to me but I bide my time

I learn about food/wine especially French wine like Latour and Saint-Émilion

I LEARN

I hang a bit with mates but again mostly stay to myself / attending university

Studying

ALWAYS studying

(*Beat*)

I did it

I got out

TIMMY

(*1980s, lights come up, age eleven, black, Timmy's smallish for his age, very bright, he's talking to a counselor in a shelter for homeless and runaway kids.*)

How come I have to live in a group home?

Why?

Why can't I live normal like other kids?

(*Voice trails off*)

You know my mother—she always used to say (*imitates her*), "Timmy / it will get better / I promise you / It will" / I believed her and I kept saying (*as if to her*) "Okay Mom / how can I help you so it can be better?"

Five years ago / we were living in the Bronx—the South Bronx. I was six then and the building we lived in—it was okay / there were a lot of drugs but our apartment was good though. We had a TV and VCR / my mom cooked and she kept the house clean and she spent a lot of time with me / and she always picked me up from school and she took care of my little sister Tessa

(*Pause*)

Me and Tessa were close—real close (*beat*) me and Tessa didn't know our dad (*tensely*) Mom said he had another family on Long Island . . . (*voice trails off*)

(*Beat*)

There were times when she got drunk and passed out and couldn't get up to make dinner so I would go in her bag and get money and buy pizza for me and Tessa

Or

Me and Tessa would have to eat cold cereal for breakfast 'cause she couldn't get up and I had to help her. There were times when she had vomited on herself and peed herself and I would try to help her clean herself up

(*Voice trails off*)

She started seeing this man named Roy

He was nice

He would buy food for us and sometimes he would cook for us and I heard him tell Mom that she should stop drinking because she had to take care of me and Tessa

Roy would take me to school sometimes and help me with my homework and Tessa loved him and called him "Daddy"

He moved in with us and Mom did stop drinking and he would take us to City Island and Coney Island and he was home with us a lot

(Beat)

When I turned seven / Roy had a birthday party for me and it was a lot of fun (slight pause) then things started to change

People would come over and they would fall asleep a lot

They would go into the bathroom and come out real sleepy

They would light a cigarette / nod / and hold their cigarette real close to the chair as they nodded and then they'd jerk up from nodding

(Slight pause)

Mom started doing that too

She started going into the bathroom / and then she'd come out and nod

She started doing it a lot and so did Roy

(Beat)

The house started getting real messy and there were always all these people and people were stealing stuff

Also she started to sell the food stamps (beat) there was boy in school and he said (*imitates him*), "My Mom said that your Mom is a no good junkie" (*becomes self*) I hit that boy for saying that (*beat*)

THEN

All these men came looking for her and she would take them in her room and they gave her money (*voice trails off*)

I was seven and even though I didn't understand everything she was doing / I knew what she doing was wrong

Tessa didn't understand / she was a baby and she saw things and imitated them. Like one time we were in the living room and I was playing with her and she said (*imitates her*), "Look Timmy / let's play this" (*becomes self*) she sticks out her arm and imitates putting a needle in her arm and then pretends to nod

Mom saw her do that

THEN Mom got into a detox program and she and Roy broke up for good and she was doing good / real good / and me, her and Tessa would laugh—man we would laugh so much / she would tickle us / kiss us . . .

I always said (*as if to her*), "Let me know how I can help you to stay clean / I'll do whatever I can"

(*Beat*)

Mom **would always promise** to STAY clean and she would for a while / but then she would start again / and there was always a new boyfriend and there were always the men she took in her bedroom

(*Pause/beat*)

I'll never forget—you know THAT day. (*Pause/beat*) Mom and another new boyfriend—his name was Johnny and they were in her room / they had a needle on the night table in a glass of water and you could see the blood in the water floating around in it

I heard Johnny say that it was his birthday and I heard Mom say (*imitates her*), "We gotta get some extra stuff so we can party" (*becomes self*) then they went out and came back and went straight to Mom's room and they didn't even close the door / I could look from me and Tessa's room into their room / I ALWAYS TRIED to keep Tessa from seeing that but I couldn't ALWAYS . . . / THAT day I put her in the living room and surrounded her with toys and put the TV on / (*slight pause*) but I ALWAYS watched / I watched Johnny—he took the needle out of the bloody water / Mom got a tie / tied his arm / then she tied her arm / took the dope / put it on the spoon / she put some of the bloody water on the spoon / lit a match / put the fire underneath the spoon / she cooked the stuff up / she shot him up first / then she drew the blood up into the needle / took a drink of gin / then shot herself up

She and Johnny put on some music / some real old stuff / like 1950s stuff / and they laid down on her bed / I was in bed watching them and this music—it was sad / A black lady with a ponytail and she had a weird voice / Mom had a whole bunch of her records / she was singing something about "My man" / anyway the music—it made me fall asleep

Then

I woke up to Mom screaming / The screams came from the living room / I ran to the living room / she was holding Tessa / Tessa wasn't moving / Mom kept screaming / just screaming / Johnny called 911 / took the rest of the dope and left—he just left (*pause/beat*) what happened was Tessa went into their room / and saw one of bags of dope opened on the night table and ate it

(*Beat*)

The police and the ambulance came and one of the ambulance workers REALLY tried to work on Tessa

This ambulance worker—he was this REAL BIG guy—he started to cry—this real BIG MAN was CRYING / he kept saying (*imitates him*), "OH MY GOD! / MY GOD! PLEASE NO!"

(*Slight pause*)

But

It was too late / Tessa was gone

(*Beat*)

Mom—she has supervised visits with me / she's always kissing me / telling me she's sorry about Tessa / saying how she wants me to live with her / she says stupid stuff like (*mockingly imitates her*), "Oh Timmy / you're growing" (*back to being self*) and I say, "Well yeah I'm eleven / I'm SUPPOSED to grow up right?" I mean I try not to be mean but . . . (*voice trails off*)

(*Slight pause*)

There are times when I JUST can't LOOK at her

(*Beat*)

I really miss Tessa

I think of her ALL the time

I ALWAYS think of that day

(*Lights change*)

One day I went into the playroom and it was sunny / a real sunny day / and I was thinking how if Tessa was with me / I would have taken her outside so we could play but also I was thinking—more like daydreaming—how nice it would be if we lived on Long Island and had a backyard with Mom and our dad

(*Beat, lights change*)

I went outside and I got on one of the swings

I began to swing really high and I was crying

One of the counselors was watching from inside and yelled out (*imitates a voice*), "Timmy stop swinging so high" (*becomes self*) and I screamed back, "No / I want to go high as I can and never come back!" / (*beat*) one of girls left her jump rope on the top bar of the swings and I kept trying to get it / I finally did / took the rope / I wrapped it around my neck / and I stood up as

I was swinging / hoping the rope would catch the top bar (*slight pause*) and I started screaming, "I WANNA BE WITH TESSA / I WANNA BE WITH TESSA / I DON'T WANNA BE HERE ANYMORE" (*speaks normally*) and I kept screaming that / and a whole bunch of people were outside by now

I just kept going higher and higher

I couldn't get the rope to wrap around the bar but thought if I swung real high I'd jump off and then that would be it (*beat*) somebody called the police and there were these firemen / they were standing on ladders surrounding me I guess to keep me from flying off or something (*beat*) I just kept yelling and crying and then I started laughing / I was laughing so hard but I don't know why because nothing was funny / but I was laughing / and crying at the same time and then I stopped laughing and just cried / I cried so hard that I couldn't see and people kept yelling (*imitates them*), "Timmy come down / PLEASE come down Timmy"

(*Pause*)

I slowed down

Then

I just sat on the swing and stopped moving and the swing finally stopped

(*Pause*)

I wonder why God is punishing me?

And sometimes (*painfully*) I HATE to say this but sometimes (*slight pause*) I HATE GOD / I KNOW it's wrong but sometimes I do

(*Pause/beat*)

I don't really want to die / I just don't want to keep feeling bad all the time

I mean I'm only eleven

I wonder where God is?

Where's God?

FLACO

Poppy gets me out of the first of the eleven group homes / Marco was in foster care then and Poppy got him back too

Mommy came home a few days later and she was on medication and things were okay

She cooked but of course Poppy cooked better 'cause he was the one who always did it and you could tell she didn't like doing it

Poppy would come home from work frontin' you know?

Sayin' shit like (*imitates him*), "The food is SO good / *Mi esposa* is a great cook / so good to have *mi familia* back / look at your mommy / isn't she beautiful and PR needs her beauty / When we get offa this stupid Coney Island and get to the REAL Boriqua / people are gonna faint when they see your mother 'cause she's so beautiful / Mommy tell the kids how you told me that I was the ONLY man for you"

(*Becomes self*)

Mommy would just look at him saying nothin' or she would say (*imitates her*), "I'm going to the boardwalk" (*becomes self*) and she would get up and leave the house

She began to do that A LOT—just GO and then when she did come back—she'd either cry or start hitting again

She began to drink because she thought with medication it would help kill the Daisy Chain voices

So she took the medication and drank and the doctors told her not to but Poppy would say (*imitates him*), "A little Chivas can't hurt" (*becomes self*) and of course it DID

She then stopped taking the medication saying she wasn't crazy and then started staying in her nightgown again and she began to look at me / (*imitates her*) "Come to me"

(*Becomes self*)

I say, "No, this needs to stop" And she says (*imitates her*), "If you don't do what the Daisy Chain King wants I'm telling Poppy you came to me"

And I can't go to another group home. And I don't want to talk to no more bullshit social workers.

And Poppy can't see nothing for what it is. Don't wanna see it.

(*Beat*)

And I ain't staying here anymore. I ain't staying. I'll break out man fucking leave here man / fucking leave

(*Pause*)

But I ain't got no money / and I ain't got no place to go / where can I go?

And I just do it to her man, I just do it to her man

(*Beat, speaks outwardly, calmly*)

One day I left school early / I just left man / I didn't feel like being there and I went to Coney with this kid Fernando I know and we went on "the Roundup" / and the rollercoaster / He told me (*imitates him*), "Yo Flaco / you could make money / there are some guys around here and all you gotta do is go under the boardwalk and touch their dicks—or they may wanna touch you / but that's it / THAT'S it bro—just TOUCH and they'll give you thirty dollars / and if you feel funny about doin' that here in Coney / you could go to the city / you know forty-nine and Broadway that place PLAYLAND where they have all the pinball games at? / Well I go there / this guy Louie—he's this older guy but he's cool / he's my friend / he sets it up and sends me out / and sent some other kids too but he know that I ain't no faggot and NONE of us are faggots / he makes SURE that them guys know they can't do nuthin more than what was agreed . . . it's good money bro / I mean it feel funny at first / somebody touchin' you or somebody's dick in your hand and then their scum in your hand—shit is nasty man but then you cop the money / wash your hands / and ditty bop on"

(*Pause, becomes self*)

I leave Fernando, I think about the money *pero* I ain't no motherfucking faggot

(*Beat*)

One day after school / me and Mommy are in my room and Poppy finds us and he jumps on ME / he starts hittin' ME / callin' ME GARBAGE / (*imitates him*), "Get out / get the fuck out / I'm gonna call that social worker and tell her / tell her you're GARBAGE"

(*Back to being self*)

So Poppy is drunk and he calls BCW and two people show up and I hear one of them say (*imitates voice*), "He's a drunk / the mother is sick and these kids are with them"

(*Becomes self*)

SO they take me AND Marco

Poppy was THEN saying (*imitates him*), "Lissen I made a mistake / nuthin happened / I made a mistake / PLEASE"

(*Becomes self*)
So Poppy called the system played HIMSELF and got played and lost me and Marco for good

So the social worker brings me and Marco to the BCW office and then they put me in Under 21 for the night / and because of Marco's age they put him someplace else

The social worker said (*imitates her*), "Flaco / you'll stay here for two days until I can get you and Marco into foster care"

What happened was I ended up stayin' at Under 21 for a week / a fuckin week

(*Beat*)

The social worker told me that because of my age—me being too old / these foster parents wanted Marco but they didn't want me (*slight pause*) and also because they had a daughter and they thought I might RAPE HER / they put it in my case folder that I WAS A DANGER SEXUALLY

(*Furious*)

In other fucking words—I get called a fuckin RAPIST

Fernando finds out where I am / Poppy told him and he comes down to Under 21 sayin' (*imitates him*), "Yo man that news is all over Coney man / I hear people talkin' about that shit ALL over the Boardwalk *pero* check it out / I know you must be goin' through a hard time stayin' here / and these kids— yo they will rip you off / niggas will steal your drawers / sneakers / hard up motherfuckas man. Lissen I can call Louie and get you outta here / remember I told you about PLAYLAND? . . . Yo it's only a few blocks away from here man and Louie got a crib where you can crash near here too / you don't have to live in the shelter man / think about it B"

(*Becomes self*)

I didn't think long / I left with Fernando and thought, "I ain't letting nobody take me for free again / I ain't givin' it away again / ain't nobody gonna play me again / I'll hustle THEM before they hustle ME"

So yeah I meet Louie / I go to Playland

(*Slight pause*)

So yeah—Playland / Louie (*sarcastically*) "HOOKS me up" and says (*imitates him*), "Flaco / I'm gonna buy you some clothes so that way not only will you look good / the trick will know how to spot you / I'll give you *chabo* to play pinball / he'll come over to you / he'll say who he is / he'll mention my name— if he DON'T / say nuthin to him—NUTHIN / if he DOES say my name / you'll know it's cool / let him go to the back FIRST / play a little more pinball for a few minutes / then go to the men's room / it'll take twenny minutes—THAT'S IT Flaco / Fernando will be around / and I'll be outside / so don't worry—we got your back

(*Becomes self*)

So this man / old white dude like forty-five comes over / I'm scared / really scared / and he mentions Louie's name and he walks to the back

(*Beat*)

I just wanna run / I just wanna break out / I play pinball / Fernando looks at me to let me know that it's time for me to go to the john

I'm walking towards the back and there are all these other kids that are there—these kids my age / and a lot of them are hustling and there are also families playin' pinball / just family hangin' out

As I walked towards the back / I wondered if the families knew what was goin' on

I get in the john / I go into the stall

This man—fuckin' pig man / fuckin' yellow teeth and he got dandruff and it's all over his coat and his skin—his skin is flaky too and he smelled like cigarettes and liquor and he was lookin' down at me sayin' (*imitates him*), "Oh Flaco / you really are Guapo/ did you know that Guapo means handsome in Spanish?" (*becomes self*) and I say, "Yeah I know" (*beat*) he unzips my pants and puts his hand on my dick man / and he keeps sayin' (imitates him), "Flaco you like it / you like it"

(*Becomes self*)

When he finished he said (*imitates him*), "Flaco I wanna see YOU again / JUST you / I'll tell Louie" (*becomes self*) then he give me an extra twenny and winks saying (*imitates him*), "The extra money is our secret" (*becomes self*) he walks out of the stall / I hear him run water in the sink / then he leaves

I stay in the stall and I started throwin' up

I go to the sink / I WASH

I just kept washing

I can't get clean enough man

(*Beat*)

I walk outside

Louie puts his around me and says (*imitates him*), "You did good Flaco / real good" (*becomes self*) and he hands me thirty dollars and of course I don't tell him about the twenny I got slipped / they take me back to Louie's crib / I smoke weed for the first time and I drink some vodka

That was my first time getting high, man

So yeah I got laid at twelve and then I got high at twelve and copped my first hustle

(*Beat*)

I got tired of Louie taking money

He was giving me and everybody else thirty and he's copping like three hundred EACH from us / one day I say to him (*as if to him*), "Louie man / you make mad money offa us and we get like only thirty?"

(*Outwardly*)

He hit me

He jumped on top of me and started hittin' / the other kids were scared / and even though they felt the same way / they didn't say shit

Man I left the crib / started turning tricks on my own

I started trickin' in the West Village

I'd get a room when I could

I'd sleep in the street or go to shelters and then leave the next day

They would put me in group homes and I'd leave them too

I would never let nobody run me again man

If I got to sell myself man / I'll be my OWN pimp

(*Pause/beat*)

This one night I had a real rough trick

This motherfucker just kept takin' me

He just kept takin' me from the ass man

He was big

Not just his dick but HE was a big dude

He said (*imitates him*), "You little **SPIC** / like me in your ass like this / you **SPICS** like to fuck / you don't like me callin' you that / too fuckin bad / I'm a mean white motherfucker, right?"

(*Becomes self*)

And

I HAD to take it man

He **KNEW** I had to take it 'cause he was so much bigger than me and plus his driver was in the car

He took me in the back of his limo

The driver had the radio on / was reading the paper

So the john finishes / throws me the money and says (*imitates him*), "Get the fuck outta my car"

(*Becomes self*)

He was this businessman

The kinda NIGGA who had some pretty wife and kids somewhere on the Upper East Side or in Westchester

If I was to tell people how many guys like that come cruising—people wouldn't believe me

Sometime you get cruised with them and their girlfriends or wives and you do threesomes

(*Beat*)

He throws four hundred dollars at me

I NEVER made that much man

I went and got a room

I bought some weed / wine

I bought some bandages and stuff

I was bleedin'

I was bleedin' bad man

I was sick man

Sick of all of it man

Him callin' me a Spic

Fucking two years on the street

And him givin' me the MOST money I ever made and me doin' nuthin when he called me a Spic

(Beat)

Getting four hundred dollars / the most I ever made

All for bein' a Spic

A no good dirty Spic whose first fuck was his own moms and who nobody believes

Four hundred dollars for ALL that man

Four hundred dollars to take it up the ass and bleed

Man I just wanted to die, man

I just wanted to be GONE

I mean I had just turned thirteen man . . .

TENNY

(*White, late fifties or early sixties, he's sitting in a jail cell but audience doesn't realize it at first.*)

My nephew Sean—God could that kid swim. My brother taught him to swim when he was only a few months old.

I mean he went straight from his mother's womb to the ocean. My brother laughed and said (*imitates him*), "Hell Sean went from one ocean to another!" . . .

(*Becomes self*)

Do you know that by the time Sean was six—he was an expert swimmer? He and his little friends formed a swimming group! I mean these little kids—four little boys met every Saturday and swam! . . .

He didn't care how cold it was. Here was this six-year-old who told my brother (*imitates him*), "Dad-I-want-to-swim-and-be-a-professional-swimmer-when-I-grow-up-and-my-friends-do-too-and-I-know-we-live-in Sag-Harbor-and-it-gets-cold-but-if-you-and-my-friends'-parents-find-a-place-for-us-to-keep-swimming-we-will-be-famous!"

(*Becomes self*)

My brother said he couldn't believe how Sean was so bold and ambitious at six! . . . Neither could any of us and all us would go to watch these kids swim . . . These funny little boys / these string bean boys take that water / move through it / push it back / embrace it

I mean there was NOTHING they couldn't do in water . . . nothing

They made water THEIRS

They moved their bodies / they OWNED their bodies

These strong / string bean / little boys / little men

(*Slight beat*)

I wonder where it came from . . . not just the swimming but the boldness and the confidence that Sean had. I mean sometimes my sister-in-law would say to Sean (*imitates her*), "Sean stop showing off" (*becomes self, angry*) and he wasn't showing off / he WASN'T / he found something he loved or better yet—what he loved was embedded in him / it was THERE / He was BORN with it . . . she—my sister-in-law—has no patience for people who are different. I mean anything outside of her cramped / silly world does not exist . . .

I am aware of what is within people and I was aware of Sean and how he would say to me (*imitates him*), "Uncle Tenny I'm NOT showing off Uncle Tenny / I just feel good in water and I feel good when the water touches my skin / what's the matter with feeling good?"

(*Becomes self*)

And

I'd say to him (*as if speaking to him*), "There is nothing wrong Sean. NOTHING. Don't listen to ANYONE that puts you down" (*back to audience*) and he grabbed me and hugged me and said (*imitates him*), "Thanks Uncle Tenny" (*becomes self, back to audience*) He called me "Tenny." See my name is actually Terence but when Sean was very little he couldn't say "Terence"—it came out "Tenny" so thus "Uncle Tenny."

He had just come from swimming practice and I was babysitting him

And

He ran to the car / threw the door open and grabbed me saying (*imitates him*), "Uncle Tenny / Uncle Tenny / I'm so happy! Take me for ice cream / PLEASE let's get some ice cream (*becomes self*) and I said (*as if to him*), "Sean you just came from swimming plus it's twenty-eight degrees / aren't you cold?" (*back to audience*) and he said (*imitates him*), "I don't care about it being cold Uncle Tenny / I love to swim anytime and I love ice cream anytime."

(*Becomes self, beat*)

So

We drive to a Dairy Queen and we get ice cream and as I'm driving towards the house / he's telling me about how he knows he's getting stronger (*imitates him*), "Uncle Tenny—you know next year when I turn seven I'm gonna be so much faster! I bet I'll beat all my friends in the team and my backstroke is getting so much stronger Uncle Tenny!"

(*Becomes self*)

His face—it was so animated and ALIVE and then he reaches over and licks my face and I say (*as if to him*), "Sean what are you doing—I'm driving man!" (*back to audience*) and he says (*imitates him*), "You have leftover ice cream on your face and you had strawberry and I had vanilla and I want to taste the strawberry!" (*becomes self*) then—and I still had one hand on the wheel—I lean over and lick him back and say (*as if to him*), "That's right and I didn't get any vanilla!"

(*Back to audience*)

And

We both laugh and laugh

(*Beat*)

He says (*imitates him*), "Hey Uncle Tenny put on the 1910 Fruitgum Company" (*becomes self*) they were this band—bubblegum band from the 60s—and the song was "Yummy, Yummy, Yummy." He knew it because my sister-in-law always played 60s music . . .

I made a copy of it 'cause I knew Sean liked it and we're singing (*sings*), "Yummy, yummy, yummy / I got love in my tummy and I feel like lovin' you"

(*Back to talking*)

And

I tickle him and then tickle him some more

And as I tickle him / I reach under his shirt

I feel the smoothness of his chest

I move to his stomach

Tickle him again

Then

I go back to his chest

I massage his nipples

I begin to massage and pull his nipples

He moans

He moans (*does this*), "Uncle Tenny / Oh Uncle Tenny"

And

I reach down

I kiss his nipples / his boy / girl voice moaning, "Uncle Tenny / Uncle Tenny"

I keep kissing

Kissing

Licking

Him

He tastes like ice cream and salt and ocean

His skin is OCEAN

Salt

Salt ocean skin and ice cream

(*Slight pause*)

I unzip his pants

I touch his penis

And he looks down and says (*imitates him*), "Penis" (*becomes self*) but it sounds like "peanuts" and I say (*as if to him*), "PEANUTS—you mean PENIS" (*back to audience*) and he says (*imitates him*), "I said PENIS" (*back to audience, becomes self*) and I said (*as if to him*), "Sean it sounded like you said PEANUTS"

(*Back to audience*)

And

Again

We laugh

(*Pause*)

I turn him over

I kiss his back

I kiss and kiss his back

I lick his back

And

He laughs

(*Beat*)

I part his legs

A child DOES have sexual feelings and they KNOW what they feel / HOW they feel so if a child I find beautiful and who ALSO finds me beautiful wants to reach for me . . . How can that be wrong?

It's HUMAN and we should not turn our backs on what is human

(Beat)

Again I know for the MOST part that this does NOT always apply—if the child does not want it, if the adult forces him, it is predatory. I would never do that.

(Pause)

I get off of Sean

There is blood

I try to wipe away the blood

He pushes me away

He cries

I say (as if to him), "Do you want to go back to the Dairy Queen?"

He looks at me and says (imitates him), "Take me home"

I drive him home

He sits in the passenger seat rocking back and forth

(Beat)

I didn't mean to cause him pain

(Beat)

He runs out of car / into the house

My sister-in-law and brother are home

I don't drive away

I don't know why

My brother runs to my car

He pulls me out of the car

He punches

Kicks me

I don't fight back

(*Beat*)

In court / I plead guilty

Family members look at me like I'm a piece of garbage

People cannot help the way they're born—they can't / I mean there is no pre-requisite for genetics and conditioning / so whoever—whatever the powers are that be / who / whatever that is / THAT's where it ALL lays

(*Slight pause*)

I fight—I DO fight with myself / I do it all the time / looking at young boys and I HAVE been with a few / and there was that part of me that knew I shouldn't / I tried to fight that THING I was BORN with / I was BORN—made this way by whatever GOD/THING you want to call it

(*Pause*)

I can't help it

I cannot help it

(*Beat, lights come up and the audience sees that Tenny is in a jail cell*)

When I first got here / people asked what I was in for

I said assault—all I said was assault

Then

One day my lawyer came to see me

And

One of the inmates was on cleaning duty

And

He recognized my lawyer and knew that he specialized in child molestation cases

The others of course found out and I was attacked and taken out of GP—general population . . . they stopped calling me Tenny

They call me Tenia

And

I guess that's what I am

A *tenia*

A worm

(*Lights fade*)

IAN

(*The bass line of Lou Reed's "Walk on the Wild Side" comes on.*)

I needed to get out of London

I was CHOKING

I really felt like I was choking

I wanted MORE

(*Slight pause, beat*)

NEW YORK

(*Quoting song*)

A hustle here, a hustle there. New York City's the place where.

Hey babe, take a walk on the wild side.

New York City's the place INDEED

Places that stayed open twenty-four hours!

Chatting up all these girls because they love my accent / I had so many women the first four years I got here

They'd ask me to say words like (*does American accent*) "Can't" and then of course I'd say (*British accent*) "Can't" and others words like (*repeats British accent*) "Dynasty" / (*repeats British accent*) "Anthony"—THEY practically wet themselves

(*Beat*)

Here in the States

I continue my studies

I study day and night

I graduate

I graduate with flying colors

Get a GREEN CARD / work as a clerk for Pricewaterhouse but it pays shit so I work construction on the side, no union, no taxes

I share a flat in the East Village with a bunch of blokes from England / Ireland / Scotland—if we were back home / we'd have nothing at all to do with one another

All they did was work / then go to bars every night and SHAG—or SAY they shagged—that's ALL they did / stinking of whiskey and lager / telling whiskey lager lies

(*Pause, beat*)

I would take these long walks

I would walk from the Village to the Upper East Side

I would walk fast

Really fast

Then slow

I slowed down as I got to those Upper East Side blocks

I loved how quiet it was

I would get there and take in ALL the buildings

I would watch people enter the building with DOORMEN

I loved the ease / the sense of KNOWING that a door **SHOULD** be open to you and WILL be

I saw how people actually walked slower and moved differently then the people downtown

I took in how clean the streets were

I would see / STUDY well-dressed people

I would look them in the eye

And

As I stared at them I thought, "That's right / SEE ME / I want you to SEE me / ONE DAY I'll be living HERE"

Then

I'd walk back downtown

I'd walk very slow

I wanted to delay going back

I was so aware of how the streets changed

Or

How the level of noise heightened

As I got closer to the East Village / I could smell the smells

Urine

The stench of cigarettes and booze

The smells of cheap food

I'd look at the council flats—housing projects as you say here in the States— and from the open windows or on the streets I'd hear / see people fighting / crying / pissed or stoned. So I got out of there. I got a place up in Murray Hill.

Got a job at Deloitte as an accountant

I said to myself / "You're not there YET Ian but you're CLOSE"

(*Beat*)

THEN

I meet HER—THE ONE

Christmas party at the firm

She's gorgeous and nice

Comes from Greenwich, Connecticut

And

She looked at ME

She didn't look about to see if everyone was looking at her 'cause she knew she looked good

She looked at ME and smiled

(*Beat*)

I couldn't believe she looked at ME

The other blokes in the room were more established than ME

They CAME from money

She looked at ME

(*Beat*)

We did great/crazy things

Went to Coney Island at night

She'd have midnight suppers that she cooked and we'd dress up!

It was great

(*Beat*)

Sleeping with her—it was fantastic

We'd make love for hours

I told her about Mum and Da

I never felt like this way about anyone

(*Beat, almost a whisper*)

I kept thinking about how one day she'd leave

I KNEW one day she would

I wondered if she laughed at things I told her

Or

If she told other people—like her girlfriends—about what I told her about Mum and Da

I HATED that I liked her

(*Slight pause*)

One day I said (*as if to her*), "You know if you ever want call it quits / or if you want see other blokes—fine by me"

(*Back to audience*)

And she looks at me like I'm mad and says (*imitates her*), "Ian I'm in love with YOU"

(*Becomes self*)

And

I love hearing that

And

I hate hearing that

(*Slight pause*)

I don't know what to do with that

(*Beat*)

I never say it back

I buy flowers

I buy perfume

But

I couldn't say it

I couldn't say it back

(*Beat*)

I met her family / went to Greenwich and had dinner / the dinnerware ALONE
was more than my rent

(*Beat*)

They were very nice, her family / very welcoming

Her mother kept refilling my plate

There were jokes / family stories and they made a point to include me

Her parents invited me to come back

And my girlfriend—she smiled

(*Beat*)

I felt like I didn't belong

I felt like ANY moment someone would say, "We see through you / you dumb MICK / you're rubbish / YOU'RE stupid / you'll NEVER belong."

(*Beat*)

I want her more than ever now but I'm petrified

(*Beat*)

We'd be out on the double dates say and maybe we went to dinner and the check would come and I'd say, "Let the rich girl from Greenwich pay"

And

She'd feel bad

And a couple of times / she got up and walked away

I grabbed her by the arm / pulled her back

I'd grab her and pull with such force it sometimes would leave a mark

(*Pause*)

I'd see the black and blue mark on her arm

I couldn't STAND seeing it

I'd feel like shit for doing that

I'd buy her flowers . . .

(*Beat*)

NOW I get promoted to senior accountant / I move to the east sixties

Doormen open/close/hold doors for ME

NEW YORK IS MINE

FINALLY MINE

She talks about us living together

I change the subject

She throws a promotion party for me / surprise party at my place / EVERYBODY from the firm is there / there's loads of food she cooked and she's looking great / and she kisses me and says (*imitates her*), "Ian I am so proud of you"

(*Becomes self, beat*)

There was a girl—a secretary—who was there and I was dancing with her and my girlfriend was dancing with another bloke—it was a great party / loads of fun

(*Beat*)

She got the Saint-Émilion. The wine I had served in the restaurant in London. I knew it went WELL with crudités.

I know I shouldn't but I HAD to have this wine

I broke my own rule

I had two glasses of wine

I got pissed on those two glasses

I go to the loo / I'm hot / sweaty / and I throw water on my face / The girl—the secretary—comes in / and next thing you know / I got her against the sink fucking her / I mean I don't even know HOW / WHY that happened / and next thing you know my girl comes in and I look over at her and just stare at her and I start to laugh . . . (*voice trails off*)

The secretary runs out

My girlfriend says (*imitates her*), "Hurry back / there's a room full of people"

The rest of the party / she's quiet and pretending to smile / serving people

The party ends

Now it's just me and her and she says to me (*imitates her*), "Ian—WHY did you do that / WHY?" (*becomes self*) and I say, "'Cause she meant shit to me that's why"

And GOD how I want drop to my knees / I want to beg her to forgive me but instead I say, "You HATE me now don't you?" / and she says (*imitates her*), "NO / I just don't understand you / I don't"

(*Becomes self*)

I look at her / and I say (*as if to her*), "YOU sit there so holier than thou / I can see you looking at me thinking I'm shit / YOU thinking you're better than ME MS. GREENWICH, CONNECTICUT" (*becomes self, back to audience*) and she says (*imitates her*), "Ian STOP / I'm not thinking that at all / why do you ALWAYS do this?"

(*Becomes self, some sort of light change happens. Note: in his exchange with girlfriend, accent should be an Irish accent, specifically a Belfast accent like his father's.*)

And I grab her and I rave / I fucking RAVE (*as if to her*), "Let me tell YOU something lady / YOU ARE THE ONE THAT IS SHIT / YOU ARE ONE THAT'S NOTHING / YOU ARE NOTHING—DO YOU HEAR ME?—YOU ARE NOTHING / NOT ME!"

(*Becomes self*)

And she says (*imitates her*), "WHAT THE FUCK IS THE MATTER WITH YOU?! YOU'RE BEING CRAZY / STUPID!"

(*Becomes self, back to audience, quietly*)

I yank her up by her shoulders and shake her and she's crying / I shake her saying, "FUCK YEW YOU'RE THE ONE THAT'S NUTTIN / RICH CUNT CALLING ME STOOPID?"

She breaks away from me and tries to run out of the flat . . .

(*Slight pause, music that could possibly come up in a loop is David Bowie's "Repetition"*)

I grab her before she gets to the door / I knock her down / pull her by the collar of her dress and I'm dragging her across the floor and she's screaming / screaming her head off / and I'm kicking her / kicking her as I drag her across the floor

I get her to the window—it's open and I push her torso out / with my knee in her chest and I say (*as if to her*), "I SHOULD FOOKIN PUSH YEW / I REALLY SHOULD"

"YEW REALLY THINK YER SOMETHING!—YEW REALLY DO / THERE ARE PRETTIER GIRLS THAN YEW / THERE ARE! / SAY IT / I WANT TO HEAR YEW SAY 'IAN I'M NOT THAT PRETTY' / SAY IT / FOOKIN SAY IT"

She says (*imitates her*), "IAN I'M NOT THAT PRETTY"

(*Becomes self*)

I say (*as if to her*), "SAY IT AGAIN"

(*To audience*)

AGAIN

She says (*imitates her*), "IAN I'M NOT THAT PRETTY"

(*Becomes self*)

Then I say (*as if to her*), "THAT'S RIGHT / YER NOT / and don't play fucking martyr with me / Yew MADE me do this / YEW DID / So go on leave me 'cause you ALWAYS wanted to anyway / I KNEW YEW WOULD—GO ON—GET FOOKIN OUT!"

(*Back to audience*)

She runs past me and leaves

(*Long beat*)

(*Goes back to speaking normally*)

I break up the flat after that / I just tear it apart / I remember doing it but as I was doing it / it wasn't real / it was like a part of me was standing outside watching

When I woke up the next morning / I was lying in the center of the sitting room still dressed and then when I looked at what I done—the state of that room—and then I thought about what I did to HER . . .

(*Beat*)

I left messages

I sent candy / perfume / she sent them back

On the cards I wrote "I LOVE YOU"

I did write it on the card

I did write "I LOVE YOU"

(*Lights fade on him*)

MIKE

In the shelters a lot of the time / your co-worker calls in sick and/or the cook doesn't show up which means the phones are ringing off the hook / when new kids come on in YOU have to do the intakes for the new kids as well as cook dinner and do individual and group counseling

You have to do this ALL ALONE

(*Slight pause*)

TODAY was one of those days

(*Beat*)

I got yet ANOTHER rejection letter from a grant

This year I thought I was going to get it

And

I just sit there—gutted

I was just gutted man

(*Beat*)

So I get to work today and like I said I'm working the tour alone. I told the kids that I really needed them to behave / I said (*as if to them*), "Look I'm working alone / totally alone today / also you know how I keep applying for grants for my writing / well this grant that I was banking on fell through so I really need for you guys to be cool"

(*Back to audience*)

There was this one kid who was a little younger than the rest named Jimmy / he's nine as opposed to eleven. The shelter housed kids ages eleven to seventeen. His father brought him in two weeks ago begging us to keep Jimmy because HE was homeless and did not want Jimmy on the streets with him.

Jimmy kept acting up / saying (*imitates him*), "YO MIKE / WHERE DO YOU

GET YOUR SHOES FROM MAN / THE NINETY-NINE-CENT STORE? YO, MAN I'M A CALL YOU 'NINETY-NINE-CENT MIKE'"

(*Becomes self*)

I kept saying (*as if to him*), "Jimmy I need for you to behave man / I really do"

(*Back to audience*)

And he would stop for a while and then would keep at ME AGAIN

Finally I yelled (*as if to him*), "GODDAMNIT, YOU'RE ON RESTRICTION FOR THREE DAYS / GO TO YOUR ROOM RIGHT NOW!"

(*Back to audience*)

He yelled (*imitates him*), "YOU AIN'T MY FATHER MAN! / I AIN'T DOIN' NUTHIN' YOU TELL ME / LOOK AT CHOO WIT YOUR NINETY-NINE-CENT CLOTHES / FUCK YOU"

(*Back to being self*)

He also bragged how he KNEW we couldn't discharge him from the shelter because of his father and because he was so young

He KEPT saying (*imitates him*), "Yo Ninety-nine-cent Mike / you can't put me out / YO Ninety-nine / wit yo ninety-nine-cent clothes"

(*Back to being self, beat*)

Finally I said (*as if to him*), "Jimmy / man you are really, really trying my patience and yeah what I'm going to do is call my supervisor and have them tell your father that you HAVE to go / I'll call special services and have them get you and bring them down to the office and out of HERE!"

(*Back to audience*)

Then

Jimmy BELLOWS (*imitates him*), "NINETY-NINE-CENT MIKE / CAN'T GET A

GRANT FOR YOUR STUPID WRITIN' / ALL OF US LAUGH AT THAT SHIT / AN YO MOMS BEIN' A HOE / YOU A STUPID NIGGA WIT A HOE FOR A MOMS / DAT'S WHAT I'M A CALL YOU / NINETY-NINE-CENT NIGGA TRICK BABY MIKE"

(*Pause, becomes self*)

I lock the office door

I grab him

The phone is ringing nonstop

The other kids have gotten quiet

I put him across my knee

I spank him

I spank / I yell, "CALLING ME A NIGGER TRICK BABY / I'M NOBODY'S TRICK BABY / I'M NOBODY'S NIGGER / I'M TIRED OF PEOPLE TREATING ME THIS WAY / I TRY / NO ONE SEES THAT / HOW I TRY/ I'M TIRED OF GETTING KNOCKED DOWN / I'M TIRED OF GETTING PASSED OVER / I'M TIRED / NO MORE / NO GODDAMN MORE!"

I keep spanking him

Jimmy is fighting back tears but the pain is too great

He tries to bite my thigh / I yank his head back / get a grip on his neck and spank harder

He screams through clenched teeth

He does not want to give in

But

THE PAIN I'M INFLICTING IS JUST TOO GREAT

Jimmy screams (*imitates him*), **"STOP MAN STOP"** (*becomes self*) and I hit harder and harder / I hit until my hand begins to hurt / I push him off my lap

(*Pause*)

(*Back to audience, speaks normally but he's shaken*)

I open the office door

Jimmy runs to his room and cries himself to sleep

The other clients hurry to their rooms

I didn't have to make them go to bed like I normally did

They ALL just went

My co-worker comes on for the next shift

I tell her what happened

She says (*imitates her*), "Good / he had it comin' and remember his father said we could spank him 'cause he can be difficult"

(*Becomes self*)

I tell her what went on for the rest of the shift / and hand her the minute book where we kept records of our shift . . . (*slight pause*) of course I did not write that I hit Jimmy / I wrote he acted up . . .

(*Pause, beat, speaking as if almost in a trance*)

Yes his father gave permission to spank but you're NOT supposed to hit / It's WRONG to hit / It's wrong . . . (*voice drops*)

See the thing is I KNOW / I KNOW how kids are / I've worked in runaway shelters for years / I know how kids will try you / test you . . . I KNOW this

(*Beat*)

I know / as much as anybody KNOWS / I come from the 'hood / I got my ass kicked by my parents / I SHOULD KNOW

When I sit down with the kids / I ALWAYS tell 'em "I DID IT / SO CAN YOU" . . .

I always say (*as if to a kid*), "We are here in BED-STY and I'm from Bed-Sty but you don't have to succumb to the street"

But you do succumb because it's all you've known/seen / the slap/punch/kick and the high

The touch/kiss/caress is not real and no one ever showed you more

There was some who did not want to show you more

Who wanted to keep you in your place

Worse yet / there are many who don't see/can't see / WANT TO SEE / you

They know your story / they THINK they know your story

They sum you up in a short glance and walk on by

You're dirty—they're not

You're fat—they're not

You smoke, you drink, you shoot—they don't

Can they smell your stench and realize the STENCH, rejection, is coming from them?

Did they watch you draw on the crack pipe and fill up on IT, CONTEMPT, in their lungs?

Did they watch you cook up and shoot and feel IT, PITY, in their veins?

As you nod in the land of a thousand nods?

And when the cold hits on a coatless night

Did they feel the WIND, APATHY, on their skin and shiver?

This is what I wanted to scream on paper

I was gonna help / I was gonna make a change / give them—the kids—a voice—make a change

How could I lose my cool like that?

How?

EPILOGUE

It doesn't all have to be black n blue

You can walk your walk

Walk it well

You can bebop

You can Brooklyn

Manchester

Boriqua

You can sidestep

And

Walk straight

You can walk a rearranged walk

Not a hustler's walk

Or

The panther like moves from the council flat walk

Or

The hard bop of Junius Street Brooklyn walk

Or

The rigid straight back poised pose of the upper-crust / Upper West Side walk

It's a walk that has an ease

You don't know where you're going

But

You know you have to get there

And

When

You get there / you want to be pure

And

Every once in a while

The black n blue will turn its trick

And memories of sore nights and wasted days hit

And

there are always the machete voices

But

You remember your back

And

You remember to straighten that back

And

You walk

You pace that walk

And

You keep walking

You walk straight

Go on

Keep walking

Go

Go

Gone

Gold

Keep walking

There's no more black n blue

It's gold

Gold

It's all gold

(*Moby's "Beautiful" plays a little louder, then fades, lights go down.*)

End of play

Printed in the United States
by Baker & Taylor Publisher Services